Twenty Poems to Bless Your Marriage

Twenty Poems to Bless Your Marriage

And One to Save It

ROGER HOUSDEN

Shambhala BOSTON & LONDON 2012

31143009653172
808.81 Twenty
Shambhala Publicati Twenty poems to bless
Horticultural Hall your marriage : and one
300 Massachusetts A to save it
Boston, Massachuse 1st ed.
www.shambhala.cor

9 8 7 6 5 4 3 2 1

First Edition
Printed in the United States of America

∞ This edition is printed on acid-free paper that meets the American
National Standards Institute z39.48 Standard.
♻ Shambhala makes every attempt to print on recycled paper.
For more information please visit www.shambhala.com.
Distributed in the United States by Random House, Inc.,
and in Canada by Random House of Canada Ltd

Designed by Lora Zorian

Library of Congress Cataloging-in-Publication Data
Twenty poems to bless your marriage: and one to save it / [compiled by]
Roger Housden.—1st ed.
p.   cm.
Includes bibliographical references.
ISBN 978-1-61180-029-6 (acid-free paper) 1. Love poetry, English. 2.
Love poetry—Translations into English. I. Housden, Roger. II. Title. III.
Title: 20 poems to bless your marriage.
PN6110.L6T84 2012
808.81'93543—dc23
2012026084

Contents

Introduction

POEMS TEACH US in ways that surpass other forms of understanding, especially when the subject concerns matters of the heart. The heart's faint whispers can often be too inarticulate for us to hear in ordinary speech. This is why poetry is so often called for on occasions like weddings, anniversaries, and Valentine's Day. Each of these life passages in its own way gives us pause to think about our lives, celebrate our loved ones, and come together in community—in the midst of everyday life.

The reason poetry is so appropriate at times like these is not merely because it fills a gap that would otherwise be left empty; it is because it manages to convey the essence of a universal human experience in a personal way. It conveys deep feeling, which is what these events all ask for, in a way that people can appreciate and understand. Good poetry is an authentic delivery of the human heart. Intimate relationships benefit from such authentic deliveries at any time of the day or night—either by one partner reading aloud to the other, across the room or down the phone, or by reading to ourselves in a quiet moment. The poems and essays in this book are intended not just for special occasions but to act as friends and guides to refer to throughout the life of a marriage.

While love is a joy that can happen in an instant, it is also a journey that can last a lifetime. Love's journey can take many forms, but among them marriage is the time-honored way that most people still choose to affirm their love for each other in the presence of their community.

Because it takes place over time, marriage, like life, passes through seasons and stages, peaks and valleys. This book illuminates and celebrates some of these major stages and provides not only inspiration for the journey but also solace and wisdom through the poems of great poets from around the world. Each of the five themes—The Joy, The Journey, The Work, The Love, The Union—begins with an essay that reflects on this particular aspect of the journey, which is then illustrated by four poems. The combination of reflective prose and poetry is intended to form an inspirational guidebook as much as a volume of poetry.

The first theme, **The Joy,** celebrates the awakening of love between two people and their commitment to that love through marriage. My essay begins by reflecting on a glorious poem by Rumi, which is one of the most ecstatic and tender declarations of love I have ever heard. The poems here rejoice in the awe and delight of love. Roy Croft ends this section with his simple and tender poem, which begins

I love you
Not only for what you are
But for what I am
When I am with you.

The Journey is prefaced by these lines from William Carlos Williams:

So different, this man
And this woman:
A stream flowing
In a field.

Marriage is a paradox, then; one in which two people are distinct individuals and yet one living stream. To discover how these apparently irreconcilable qualities can thrive together is a lifelong journey, one that is full of impossible quandaries, laughter, and sparks of grace that can suffuse the most humdrum moments of family life.

The Work comes when, sooner or later, two people consciously choose to turn their shared suffering and challenges into material for their own growth and for the deepening of the relationship. The work begins by delving deep into oneself, D. H. Lawrence tells us. When we choose to explore our pain rather than run from it, uncomfortable as it may be, it uncovers a kind of joy in marriage that cannot be found outside of it, says Denise Levertov, in "The Ache of Marriage":

> looking for joy, some joy
> not to be known outside it
>
> two by two in the ark of
> the ache of it.

We see, as in Clare Shaw's "Vow," that the difficulties that arise in our lives can make our love and commitment to each other stronger.

The Love in a long-term relationship can express itself in many ways, and in this section I explore two main themes that may weave through a relationship from beginning to end. The first is kindness; a compassionate love that Hafiz, in his poem "It Happens All the Time in Heaven," tells us is a desire to wish and also work for the other's good. Shakespeare, in "Sonnet 116," develops this by saying that a true marriage is one of *true minds*—in the Platonic sense of a meeting of minds that hold the same ideals.

This more exalted form of love, which the Greeks called *Agape*, is accompanied in a successful marriage by a thread of subtle fire that we can call the realm of Eros. Eros, god of desire—not only sexual desire but the desire for connection, for a shared life—brought the couple together in the beginning, and through the years rises and falls in varying intensities. Stephen Dunn's poem in this section is a joyous acknowledgment of his need for that connection, and the last poem in this section, "We Take the New Young Couple Out to Dinner," shows it alive and well in later years.

The Union that is gradually forged through years of marriage is different from the feeling of union that accompanies the joy of the wedding day. That first joy is often one of enchantment, which time has to temper and mature with the trials of daily life. The union described in Robert Bly's "A Third Body" is of a different order. There is no deeper presence of being that can move between two people than emerges from the quiet air of this poem. The scene is completely ordinary, two people sitting near each other, talking or not talking. Yet with or without words, the underlying rest and silence remain undisturbed.

They obey a third body that they share in common.

For an enduring union to thrive, a level of comfort and understanding is reached in the realm of Eros as well. Wendell Berry's "The Blue Robe" describes the deep pleasure of a couple who have known both these qualities for a lifetime together.

The book ends with a further section called **The Saving Grace**, which consists of a selection from just one poem, "Listening to the Köln Concert," by Robert Bly. If there is one thing that is necessary for the health and longevity of a marriage, it is the willingness to accept imperfection, both in one's partner and in oneself. Bly's poem speaks to this in the most poignant and tender way I have ever read.

My role as a curator of the poems you find in this volume is to find those voices that can speak to contemporary concerns and aspirations relating to marriage in a way that is a direct communication from heart to heart, from poet to reader; that is not just inspiring but revelatory, casting new light and feeling on the matters of our own lives.

I know from my experience writing the Ten Poems series that it is important for the poems to convey a depth of meaning in an inspiring and also accessible way. Many people find poetry intimidating, and all too often a reminder of school. Far from being a poetry professor, I am glad to be an amateur—a word whose roots lie in the Italian *amatore*, a "lover." My own interest lies not in any academic realm but in exploring the deeper currents of life; and that interest has taken me in the last decade or so to poetry. So it is by virtue of my amateur status (a venerable English, if not American tradition) that the poems that most easily capture my own attention are those with an accessible style and language. Perhaps the only exception in this volume is Shakespeare's "Sonnet 116". But Shakespeare is timeless, and this sonnet carries such universal appeal—especially for those who are married or about to be married—that I found it impossible to leave him out.

It is my wish that this little book may serve as a lamp to light your way along the intimate path—which will sometimes be rocky, sometimes smooth; sometimes dark and sometimes like a summer day—that leads two separate people into a shared love and ultimately, to a communion not only of the body but also of the spirit.

I

The Joy

Lovers don't finally meet somewhere.
They're in each other all along.

—RUMI

✎ THE RECOGNITION

I HAVE FAITH IN THE VALUE of love's enchantment; the rich colors the world takes on in lovers' eyes. I believe in the tears of love, the joys of love, in the warmth in the chest that comes when we feel we have known this person all of our lives and beyond. The recognition: it is what we long for.

You may say that this is nothing more than delusion; that an enchantment necessarily deceives and leaves us disappointed and possibly lonely. This is why love is so often cast as a spell, one that earlier cultures have seen as a curse that brings only ill fortune and even death. Think of Tristan and Isolde, Lancelot and Guinevere, Abelard and Heloise, and countless other ill-fated lovers who blaze a path through our mythology and literature. Think of Romeo and Juliet.

Yet these are all tales of illicit love, and these lovers never had the opportunity to grow beyond love's season of enchantment. They transgressed the religious, moral, or social boundaries of their time. When the fire of love enters the container of marriage, the enchantment becomes just one stage on love's journey. In marriage, the enchantment can become the fuel for something greater than itself, for the creation of a life larger than one's individual ambitions.

For all the challenges it may bring in distinguishing reality from imagination, the romance of love is one of the deepest and most integral experiences of being human. It is a gift from beyond the strategies of the self-seeking mind. It may upset the status quo, and sometimes the social order. It doesn't come on demand; rather it chooses us if it is so inclined, even if it may be inconvenient to our best-laid plans. It suspends our judgment, a rare experience in itself, and one that generates a liberating relief as well as a rare absence of self-preservation. A wholehearted, full-blown romantic love is one without conditions: no dowry, no big bank account, no promising job, no plastic surgery necessary. Even though you may point to the many qualities of your partner, this kind of love seizes us for its own. It is a gift that defies explanation.

A love like this is often called divine precisely because it comes from a region outside of our conscious minds. It is a mystery that fills us with an elation, a joy, a sense of life and meaning beyond and larger than our ordinary lives. It joins us not only to our beloved but to life as a whole, and even, if we think that way, to God. The great eleventh-century Sufi mystic Ibn Ibn 'Arabi writes:

> It is God who in each loved one manifests himself to the gaze
> of each lover . . . for it is impossible to adore a being without
> imagining the divinity present in that being. . . . Thus it goes
> for love: a creature really loves no one but his Creator.[1]

Throughout the ages mystics of all religions have described their experience of God in terms of a lover, and perhaps no one more so than the great Persian poet and mystic Rumi. Rumi fell in love with God through another human being, a wild, unorthodox, wandering Sufi known as Shams. Rumi has become widely known in the West in the last twenty years, above all, I think, because of his ability to write sublime and ecstatic love poetry; poetry that can be taken to refer equally to God or to Shams, his beloved teacher. For Rumi, God lives in the human heart, and when the heart loves, it is because it recognizes the divine in the other, mortal human being. The fruit of that recognition is joy, and the poem by Rumi that begins this section cries joy from the very first lines:

> From the beginning of my life
> I have been looking for your face.
> But today I have seen it.

He then goes on to proclaim that

> Your effulgence
> has lit a fire in my heart
> And you have made radiant for me
> the earth and the sky.

The love he is trying to express in words is simply beyond all categories:

> I am ashamed to
> call this love human
> And afraid of God
> to call it divine.

Today, in a less orthodox world than thirteenth-century Persia, we would surely not feel ashamed to declare that our love has allowed us to see the divine—though we might call it the soul, or the nobility of soul—in the face of our beloved. Such terms as these can still stagger from our lips, not from deference to some religious belief but rather from a spontaneous stirring of the heart that has no other words to express what it feels. I recently had the privilege to recite this poem of Rumi's for a couple at their wedding ceremony as they looked into each other's eyes. Of all the poems they searched through for the occasion, this was the one that expressed most directly their feelings for each other.

When this joyous love from beyond has the great good fortune to be brought to earth in a marriage ceremony, it provides the fuel and the motivation to ride the inevitable challenges that all couples encounter when they set out together on the conjugal life.

Whereas a love like this begins with unknowing—where it came from, why this person and not that one, what its purpose may be in our lives—a marriage proposal is formed from a knowing. You just know, with a knowing of the heart, and not of the rational mind, that this is the person you want to spend your life with. It's not so much that you make a commitment as you recognize and affirm that a commitment is already there in the quality and nature of your being together. To bring forth that recognition in words brings it down to earth, out of the realm of possibility and into actuality. This is an ennobling moment, because it promises to bring the spirit of the divine to dwell among the physical, moral, and social constraints of being human. It is an act of courage on both people's parts.

Not only that, Jane Hirshfield suggests in her beautiful poem "A Blessing for Wedding," a marriage ceremony also joins two people in the eyes of the whole world—not just the assembled guests but all that is blossoming and flowering and also dying within it at the very moment that the couple exchange vows and rings. Everything is connected, she is saying, even as everything is constantly changing. Just as you are gazing into each other's eyes and slipping a ring on each other's finger, you are in some way synchronizing with everything else that is also being born, bursting into life, and falling from the tree at the very same time.

In the act of marriage, her poem tells us, you are joining the great circle of creation, and you yourselves may contribute to that circle in other ways than if you were still alone; not only with children but also through the joy of your union and even creative acts inspired by *the marriage of true minds*, as Shakespeare says in the sonnet included later in this book.

And although a vow can sound like something written in stone, unchangeable and irreplaceable, Hirshfield urges us to think of it in another, more creative, enlivened way:

Let the vow of this day keep itself wildly and wholly
Spoken and silent, surprise you inside your ears.

How do you keep a vow *wildly?* I would think she means that the vow is not a literal but a living and sacred compact with a life of its own that you will grow into and discover along your way. This is why it can *surprise you inside your ears.* After all, however much you may think you know them, your marriage partner is in reality a mystery that will only gradually reveal itself through time, and even then only in part. Just as you yourself are a mystery to them, and probably to yourself also. So with marriage we are saying *Yes!* to the unknown as well as the known. Another great poet, Gabriel García Márquez, said of his wife of many years,

I know her so well that she is completely and utterly
    unknown to me.

This is why marriage is a sacred pact: we are entering a mystery.
We human beings have a wordless something within us that has been
called by a thousand names and more. We can say it is the reflection of
a distant star whose name we do not know. We can say it is the I that
we always are and have been and yet so often forget; the one who will
remain standing when we die. Whatever image we give it, that mys-
tery is the light that we see when we look into the eyes of our beloved.
Beyond their beauty, this is their true beauty; beyond their knowing,
this is their true wisdom.

Marriage is sacred when we recognize that light in our beloved,
and know that this is our way home; that while they cannot walk our
road for us, they can light our way, as we can theirs. This is what Hen-
rik Nordbrandt is alluding to in his poem "Our Love Is Like Byzan-
tium." The Byzantium he is thinking of was all turquoise and flashing
gold, all icons and fragrant incense. Throughout the poem he refers to
a glow that is to be seen on the beloved's face, a glow deeper than any
words or description. The poem ends with an astonishing last stanza:

When I turn towards you
in bed, I have a feeling
of stepping into a church
that was burned down long ago.

Astonishing, because it gathers together into one place so many
worlds, and declares with an upwelling of joy that we inhabit all of

them at the same time. The couple is in bed, in this ordinary hum-drum life where you lie down when you are tired. But they are also in church; not any church but one that was *burned down long ago*—so they have gone beyond time, to a timeless zone,

> and where only the darkness of the eyes of the icons
> has remained
> filled with the flames
> which annihilated them.

Such a deep and multilayered image, I shudder when I read it. Those icon eyes—large, impersonal, always dark, filled with flames—*the flames which annihilated them.* He is in bed, remember, gazing into his beloved's eyes, which have become an icon's eyes. An icon is a gate-way to the divine. It is the gaze of the icon that works on the person standing before it. The purpose of its gaze is to burn the ego away so that all that remains of him is the pure face of love. This lover sees all this in his beloved's eyes next to him in bed. He sees that she herself has been burned away (by their love), and all that remains of either of them is love itself.

These first three poems take the love of one human being for another down to its deepest core, which extends out beyond the individual to all the turning worlds. They take up the theme that is in the Song of Songs in the Bible, and in so much mystical poetry in all traditions—that human love is the mirror image of the love of the divine. When you read these poems in the context of marriage, they bring these exalted sentiments down to earth; down to the human expression of the wonder and joy that breaks across a person's face when they recognize and take for their own the one they have always longed for.

More commonly, contemporary culture encourages poets to use a love language that is more psychological than spiritual, though the boundary between psyche and spirit is as thin as it ever was. Spiritual growth today is often synonymous with individuation, the maturing into the person you have the potential to be. The royal and sometimes difficult road to that individuation is love itself: love of another, not for what you want them to be, or imagine them to be, but for who they are.

This is the love honored in the plain, simple language attributed to Roy Croft:

> I love you
> Not only for what
> You have made of yourself
> But for what you are helping me
> To make of myself.

He loves her, he says,

> Because you see me.

This poem has no title, but I have called it *The Recognition*. Isn't that what we all want, to be seen in our deepest core? In love we recognize not only the other, as if we have known that person all along; we also feel seen, recognized for who we are ourselves. This theme of mutual recognition echoes the more ecstatic recognition celebrated by Rumi in our first poem. Croft's poem, however, dispenses with exalted imagery and instead employs homely, everyday speech. He, like Rumi, is a man of his own time.

> I love you because you
> Are helping me to make
> Of the ruins of my life
> Not a tavern
> But a temple.

The place of worship is no longer external but within, in the human heart—as it is in Rumi's poem, but shorn here of any reference to the divine. What has changed is not so much the sentiment but the language in which it is expressed. Rumi's last lines, remember, are

> I am in the house of mercy
> And my heart
> is a place of prayer.

In Croft's poem, the lover's heart is also becoming a temple, and yet one made of the unnoticed and even discarded parts of her being. And it is being made—as a soul is "made" over a lifetime—with the help of the love shared between two people. The words of this poem themselves carry a humility and a tenderness that is the signature of this temple in the heart. *The peace that passes understanding* is another of its signs; the rightness, the *settling* that comes when you know that the person your heart has recognized is at your side. And all of this happens, not by any effort of will but rather, as the speaker says, because the beloved is being his or herself—being authentically who they are. This, in the journey of individuation—the journey of contemporary human beings—is when heaven is brought to earth. And when that happens, love can send forth its finest flowers.

Looking for Your Face
BY RUMI *translation by Fereydoun Kia*

From the beginning of my life
I have been looking for your face
but today I have seen it

Today I have seen
the charm, the beauty,
the unfathomable grace
of the face
that I was looking for

Today I have found you. . . .
I am ashamed
to call this love human
and afraid of God
to call it divine

Your fragrant breath
like the morning breeze
has come to the stillness of the garden.
You have breathed new life into me. . . .

Every fiber of my being
is in love with you

Your effulgence
has lit a fire in my heart
and you have made radiant
for me
the earth and the sky

My arrow of love
has reached its target
I am in the house of mercy
and my heart
is a place of prayer

A Blessing for Wedding
JANE HIRSHFIELD

Today when persimmons ripen
Today when fox-kits come out of their den into snow
Today when the spotted egg releases its wren song
Today when the maple sets down its red leaves
Today when windows keep their promise to open
Today when fire keeps its promise to warm
Today when someone you love has died
    or someone you never met has died
Today when someone you love has been born
    or someone you will not meet has been born
Today when rain leaps to the waiting of roots in their dryness
Today when starlight bends to the roofs of the hungry and tired
Today when someone sits long inside his last sorrow
Today when someone steps into the heat of her first embrace
Today, let day and dark bless you
With binding of seed and rind bless you
With snow-chill and lavender bless you
Let the vow of this day keep itself wildly and wholly
Spoken and silent, surprise you inside your ears
Sleeping and waking, unfold itself inside your eyes
Let its fierceness and tenderness hold you
Let its vastness be undisguised in all your days.

Our Love Is Like Byzantium
BY HENRIK NORDBRANDT *translation by* *Henrik Nordbrandt and Alexander Taylor*

Our love is like Byzantium
must have been
on the last evening. There must have been
I imagine
a glow on the faces
of those who crowded the streets
or stood in small groups
on streetcorners and public squares
speaking together in low voices
that must have resembled
the glow your face has
when you brush your hair back
and look at me.

I imagine they haven't spoken
much, and about rather
ordinary things
that they have been trying to say
and have stopped
without having managed to express
what they wanted
and have been trying again

and given up again
and have been looking at each other
and lowered their eyes.

Very old icons, for instance,
have that kind of glow
the blaze of a burning city
or the glow which approaching death
leaves on photographs of people who died young
in the memory of those left behind.

When I turn towards you
in bed, I have a feeling
of stepping into a church
that was burned down long ago
and where only the darkness in the eyes of the icons
has remained
filled with the flames
which annihilated them.

The Recognition

ATTRIBUTED TO ROY CROFT

Adapted by Roger Housden

I love you
Not only for what you are
But for what I am
When I am with you.
I love you
Not only for what
You have made of yourself
But for what you are helping me
To make of myself.
I love you
For putting your hand
Into my heaped-up heart
And passing over
All the foolish, weak things
That you can't help
Dimly seeing there,
And for drawing out
Into the light
The beautiful belongings
That no one else had looked
Quite far enough to find.

I love you because you
Are helping me to make
Of the ruins of my life
Not a tavern
But a temple;
Of the works
Of my every day
Not a reproach
But a song.
I love you
Because you see me.
I love you because
You have done more
Than any fate could
Have done to
Settle my heart.
Yet you do so
Without a touch,
Without a word,
Without a sign.
You do so because
You are you.

2

The Journey

So different, this man
And this woman:
A stream flowing
In a field.

———WILLIAM CARLOS WILLIAMS

❧ Alone Together

ANY DEEP AND INTIMATE relationship, and certainly marriage, is a metaphor for life: it is a journey whose outcome we can never know, except that one day it will end. The journey itself, then, is the adventure, whatever happens along the way; even and perhaps especially when it does not fulfill our expectations.

When the joy and the recognition that drew two people together in the first place begin to mature and deepen with the years, we become accustomed to encountering the many faces of ourselves and our beloved. In the spirit of the journey, our task and opportunity are to acknowledge whomever it is that turns up at our door—a joy, a sadness, a flash of anger. Our challenge is to embrace them all. A lasting intimate relationship is an alive and dynamic entity that will unfold its treasures and dragons over the course of time. The journey then—the flurry of days that make up our lives, with their eating and laughing and crying and wondering, with their doubts and fears and joys, their successes and failures—is all we have.

If there is any note to yourself to keep in your pocket as you set out, it is to start along the way as you mean to continue: with the faith (to recall David Whyte's poem in the last section) that your journey will take you where you need to go; that love will lead you, and not the other way around. And though the journey into love has been trodden by countless men and women before you, so that there are certain signposts along the way, each of our journeys is unique and special to us. To have faith in our love is to have faith in our own life's unfolding, and in where it wants to go. What we can be sure of is that it will not and cannot be merely a story of roses. We have only to look at the workings of our own minds to see that there are as many valleys as there are mountaintops in the course of a single day. How much more of an adventure it must be, then, when two hearts and minds travel the same road side by side.

Kahlil Gibran, in his lyrical poem "On Marriage," advises you to travel that road while allowing *spaces in your togetherness.*

Love one another, but make not a bond of love

he goes on to say. In the early joy of feeling merged in a great love, it can seem as if you would never wish to step out of the enchantment that seems to gather the two of you up into one being, free and light as air. Wherever you are, it can feel as though your beloved is there by your side, even if he or she is a thousand miles away. This is a beautiful and important stage on the journey of love, and it can return again and again over the years.

At the same time, we will always be distinct and unique individuals, with our own preferences and inclinations, our own longings and dreams. If we were to try to sustain the merging beyond its natural span, we would eventually become resentful and claustrophobic, sensing that our own life was somehow being consumed by the relationship. This is when love itself can begin to seem like a limitation on your individuality and your own unique path in life. You will always be distinct from your beloved even as you travel the same road. Part of the journey, then, is learning to be alone together, as Gibran says so touchingly in these lines:

Sing and dance together and be joyous, but let each one of
    you be alone,
Even as the strings of a lute are alone though they quiver
    with the same music.

It takes courage to walk alone together; to fully embrace your beloved into your life even as you claim your life for your own. Courage, and also discernment and insight. Yet the rewards will be great; for a true relationship can only be formed not from a merged confusion of identities but between two distinct individuals.

The last image in Gibran's poem takes up again the theme of relationship as a temple, a holy place that is constructed with pillars that

. . . stand together yet not too near together.

This image has stayed with me for decades; it is a beautiful illustration of how two people standing side by side, on their own feet and in their own individuality, can support something greater than either of them, which is the flowering of the relationship itself.

When two individuals are in an intimate relationship, rather than a merged confusion of two people, they are more likely to be able to weather the storms that will inevitably come their way. Two individuals are at some time bound to disagree. They are likely to quarrel, and probably sooner rather than later. But there is always the possibility that a space can open in their opinions and fixed positions, like a sudden break in the clouds that seems to come out of nowhere.

Conrad Aiken's poem "The Quarrel" expresses this beautifully.

It can take just a single word to break love's spell, and to have the couple,

> . . . hopeless both, yet hoping
> Against all hope to unsay the sundering word.

How easily and unexpectedly these awkward words can slip from our mouths before we have the presence of mind to say it differently:

> How, with as little sound as the fall of a leaf,
> The shadow had fallen, and lover quarreled with lover.

Aiken's poem is so tender and poignant precisely because we can feel how much these two people love each other; how, in the midst of the stony silence that follows their quarrel, with seemingly no way out of their impasse, one of them can still say

> . . . I marveled—alas, alas—
> At your deep beauty, your tragic beauty . . .

Even in the depths of their despair,

> When love no longer dared, and scarcely desired

the reader can still sense the glimmer of connection to the larger reality of the relationship itself, beyond their individual fixed positions of the quarrel. They may not know how to consciously step into that larger reality—a reality that, somehow, they still share—but they know it is there. And because of this, all is not lost. Because of this, serendipity—or call it the workings of grace—can change everything.

The next-door neighbor puts on a record and the music pours into the space, the tiny space that still remains open between them in spite of everything. Without that sliver of openness—a love now *scarcely desired,* but at least still desired in some small measure—the quarrel and their impasse may have simmered on for days or even weeks; and when it eventually faded away, it would have left a mark that over the years would have contributed to a gradual narrowing of their vision of the other. But no, the music started,

> Like the indomitable heart of life that sings
>
> When all is lost; and startled from our sorrow,
> [. . .]
> We raised remembering eyes, each looked at other,
> Blinded with tears of joy . . .

Remembering eyes: this is the key. That for whatever reason, in that moment the music made them remember again what they always knew: their joy in the love of one another. And in that moment, the quarrel becomes absurd and is forgotten.

> And we rose, to the angelic voices of music,
> And I touched your hand, and we kissed, without a word.

And yet sometimes life circumstances—not quarrels, as such, nor anything that may have sprung from the tussle of two minds—may come between us and seem to make our life together unsustainable, at least for a time. Who knows what that might be? Illness. A job offer in another city or country. Something or someone from an earlier part of our life that we have to attend to. Financial calamity. In circumstances like these, what is it that can endure? Eliza Griswold's poem "Tigers" speaks to the very heart of this question.

For whatever reason, the life that the couple in "Tigers" has promised each other is no longer possible, at least not for now.

> not for lack of wanting
> but wanting can't make it so.

What then, can they do? They are in an impossible situation. They cling to a vine at the cliff's edge. Whichever way they turn, their life awaits them in the form of a hungry tiger. Their response is

> . . . Let us love
> one another and let go.

Incredible poem! The image instantly burns itself into the mind. All the more stunning, however, is the response of the speaker to the situation, who puts faith in the essence of their relationship, which is love itself rather than any of the conditions they find themselves in, and they let go into that. Their love will live on even if the conditions of their life make it impossible for them to live in a conventional marriage. This is to live in the greater space of the relationship, whatever form it may assume. Forms can change, but a deep and abiding love is for a lifetime.

The last poem in this section, Wesley McNair's "Love Story," looks back on marriage after a number of years, and sees the beauty and grace in the small things; those ordinary, humdrum events and diffi-culties that constitute family life. These are the moments that make up the greater part of our lives, these passages of apparently insignificant acts and remarks. And yet it is precisely the minutiae of our life to-gether, rather than the grand occasion or special night out, that reveal the true color and emotional tone of the relationship.

McNair's poem follows the start of a car journey, and from the beginning the poet sees more in the ordinary event than the eye can see. All that appears to be happening is that a couple with children and dog struggle to get their old car started on a hill when the battery turns out to be dead. The husband pushes while the wife steers. But this is merely to describe the outer humdrum event. McNair turns it into poetry when he asks what it was that was opening the door to let his dog and children into the backseat of the car:

we'd parked in the driveway
next to the down-hill road because
the battery went dead the day before—
what, but a prayer?

A prayer that the car would start. A prayer that they wouldn't be late, perhaps. A prayer that the dead battery wouldn't spark an argument. A prayer, whatever the asking. A faith, then, in some greater life inher-ent in the mundane moment. It was a long time ago, and they were younger then, and probably short of resources; tempers could easily fray, especially with four kids and a dog in the backseat. And the car didn't start, and he did have to start pushing, and they did fall into arguing. But what were their arguments, he asks:

what, but an agreement to go on
despite our limitations?

All the while in this poem, there is an overarching faith in that which
is more than the details—a faith in the love these two people bear for
each other; in the poetry that lies in the passing together of ordinary
days. It is this, in the midst of their despair—

when the engine suddenly caught
and you roared away and came back
for me . . .
[. . .]
the whole family smiling

—that is the real blessing with which he brings the poem to an end.

In its own way, each of these four poems in *The Journey* weaves
the ordinary events of married life into a larger tapestry of the love
that one person has for another. This is the real nourishment for the
journey itself, wherever the journey takes you. And each poem, too,
points to the space there must be in our own minds and also between
each other to be able to embrace the bigger picture. In this spacious-
ness, the troubles along the way will seem, as McNair says—*what, but
a blessing?*

On Marriage
BY KAHLIL GIBRAN

You were born together, and together you shall be
    forevermore.
You shall be together, when the white wings of death scatter
    your days.
Ay, you shall be together even in the silent memory of God.
But let there be spaces in your togetherness,
And let the winds of the heavens dance between you.

Love one another, but make not a bond of love:
Let it rather be a moving sea between the shores of your souls.
Fill each other's cup but drink not from one cup.
Give one another of your bread but eat not from the same
    loaf.
Sing and dance together and be joyous, but let each one of
    you be alone,
Even as the strings of a lute are alone though they quiver
    with the same music.

Give your hearts, but not into each other's keeping.
For only the hand of Life can contain your hearts.
And stand together yet not too near together:
For the pillars of the temple stand apart,
And the oak tree and the cypress grow not in each other's
    shadow.

The Quarrel

BY CONRAD AIKEN

Suddenly, after the quarrel, while we waited,
Disheartened, silent, with downcast looks, nor stirred
Eyelid nor finger, hopeless both, yet hoping
Against all hope to unsay the sundering word:

While the room's stillness deepened, deepened about us,
And each of us crept his thought's way to discover
How, with as little sound as the fall of a leaf,
The shadow had fallen, and lover quarrelled with lover;

And while, in the quiet, I marveled—alas, alas—
At your deep beauty, your tragic beauty, torn
As the pale flower is torn by the wanton sparrow—
This beauty, pitied and loved, and now forsworn;

It was then, when the instant darkened to its darkest,—
When faith was lost with hope, and the rain conspired
To strike its gray arpeggios against our heartstrings,—
When love no longer dared, and scarcely desired:

It was then that suddenly, in the neighbor's room,
The music started: that brave quartette of strings
Breaking out of the stillness, as out of our stillness,
Like the indomitable heart of life that sings

When all is lost; and startled from our sorrow,
Tranced from our grief by that diviner grief,
We raised remembering eyes, each looked at other,
Blinded with tears of joy; and another leaf

Fell silently as the first; and in the instant
The shadow was gone, our quarrel became absurd;
And we rose, to the angelic voices of music,
And I touched your hand, and we kissed, without a word.

Tigers

BY ELIZA GRISWOLD

What are we now but voices
who promise each other
a life neither one can deliver
not for lack of wanting
but wanting can't make it so.
We hang from a vine
at the cliff's edge.
There are tigers above
and below. Let us love
one another and let go.

Love Story

BY WESLEY MCNAIR

What was opening the door
those years ago to let our four kids
one by one followed by the dog
into the backseat of the old compact car
we'd parked in the driveway
next to the down-hill road because
the battery went dead the day before—
what, but a prayer?

What were our arguments
as we tried to time my pushing
the family down the road and your
taking your foot off the clutch
to start the car, though instead of bringing it
to a dead stop over and over—
what, but an agreement to go on
despite our limitations?

What was the moment
in the midst of our despair
when the engine suddenly caught
and you roared away and came back
for me, and I got in by the soda can
on the floor and the dog now sitting

between us on the emergency brake,
the whole family smiling

as the trees broke apart faster and faster
above our heads—what, but a blessing?

3

The Work

Those who want to have a deep love in their lives must collect and save for it, and gather honey.

—RAINER MARIA RILKE

✣ SOAKED IN HONEY, STUNG AND SWOLLEN

HOW DIFFICULT IT CAN BE to live this human life. Our early wounds, the challenging times, the worry over what may come—the past, the present, and also the future can weigh so heavily on our hearts that we may be forgiven for thinking now and then that there will never be another dawn. Our hopes and dreams are always as fragile as leaves in the fall, for there is no knowing what life may bring; which events we would never have suspected might be there in the shadows all along. In her poem "If You Knew," Ellen Bass wonders what people would look like if we were able to see them as they are:

> Soaked in honey, stung and swollen,
> Reckless, pinned against time?[1]

I love these lines. They manage to compress the complexity and also the poignancy of human life into one utterly original, shimmering image. When two people come together, both of them *pinned against time,* life's mysterious weave of joy and suffering is made all the more intricate and subtle. Yet the challenges of two lives conjoined can provide rich soil for our own deepening and flowering; and especially when it is thick with the dark leaves of many years. For in it we may discover that there is a treasure worth digging for; one that was not so apparent in the first flush of our romance and loving.

The poems in this section take the theme of the journey to a deeper and more conscious level. Here, the journey is less upon the outer path of life than an inner one, down into the *deep old heart*, as Lawrence says in the first poem. What is required, these poems say, and each from a different angle, is not just the acknowledgment that the unexpected will happen, not just a response to the invitation to embrace life in whichever way it appears at our doorstep, but to consciously work with the material of our own marriage and also of our own inner life.

Two friends of mine have been married for forty-five years, and they enjoy each other's company now more than they ever did. If they had not told me I would never have known that they had almost parted three times over the years, and had crossed deserts in their marriage as well as fertile ground. What their marriage obliged them to do, they said, was to look at themselves in the mirror of the other, and to have the humility and also the grace to take responsibility for what they saw. Their marriage was a pact, not only to forge a life together but to forge their own individualities in its fire. Because marriage can indeed be a trial by fire, they said, as well as a source of joy.

Marriage is a crucible that commits into form the love that we have for another, and in so doing, it joins us to the passage of time. It takes our winged feet, holds them on the ground, and binds us at the ankles to the one we have chosen. Anything that finds its way into form is subject to the scrapes and dents that come with the passing of the years. Marriage is no exception, and the traditional Christian wedding vows—"for better or for worse, for richer for poorer, in sickness and in health"—spell it out: not everything we sign up for is going to make us happy. Rilke points out in one of his letters that disappointment in love often arises from false expectations:

Like so many other things, people have also misunderstood the position love has in life; they have made it into play and pleasure because they thought that play and pleasure are more blissful than work; but there is nothing happier than work, and love, precisely because it is the supreme happiness, can be nothing other than work.[2]

In another letter, he says,

It is also good to love: because love is difficult. For one human being to love another human being: that is perhaps the most difficult task that has been entrusted to us, the ultimate task, the final test and proof, the work for which all other work is merely the preparation.[3]

The work can only begin with oneself. D. H. Lawrence, in his extraordinary poem in this section, urges us to *go deeper than love, for the soul has greater depths.* He takes the importance of solitude that Gibran alludes to in his poem in the previous section, and brings the theme to a deeper, more consciously interior level. We must, I think he is saying, go deep into our own solitude to find the essence of who we are; down into our *deep old heart*, and lose sight of the usual references that make up our habitual identity—including our relationship itself. Only there shall we be on firm and honest ground, in an integrity where we can know and speak our truth in a way that honors both our own life and that of our partner. *Break the mirrors*—the mirrors in which we may have been captivated for so long by our own face—our own views, our own prejudices and opinions. We must be willing to return to zero, Lawrence is saying; and from that primal ground we may emerge into a new and authentic life, both with ourselves and with our partner.

When we take the journey down into ourselves that Lawrence is urging, we will at some stage encounter the store of grief and sorrow that lies hidden somewhere in all of us. There are opportunities we missed that may never return; opportunities to love, to create, to work, to forgive, to care, that could have made both our own lives and those of others richer and fuller. There are things we have said and done in our lives that may have caused others, including our partner, deep pain. There are losses we have sustained that may never have been fully acknowledged or grieved. The sorrow of the world surrounds us, but we may have lived as if immune to it, apparently safe in a world of our own making.

In his poem "The Well of Grief," David Whyte says that unless we go down into these dark depths, we

> will never know the source from which we drink,
> The secret water, cold and clear.

One of the great sorrows in love that must find its way into the cloth of a marriage lies in the realization that love can move in an instant from angelic bliss to abject misery. On the one hand, we are never so complete and fulfilled as when we are with our beloved. On the other hand, no one else seems so capable of opening the wound that lies deep in our own psyche. This is why the advice of Lawrence and Whyte is so crucial: the work lies in discovering that the wound hidden deep inside us is the same wound that is deep in the other.

Our beloved serves to show us what we do not easily want to see or acknowledge in ourselves. Our feelings of hurt, of rage, of terror arise not from them but from deep within us. To own and embrace the wounds in our inner depths is first and foremost a solitary work, but the joy of it follows when its fruits are shared with the beloved. Rilke, in his essay "On Love and Other Difficulties," tells us that

> Love is at first not anything that means merging, giving over and uniting with the other. . . . It is a high inducement to the individual to ripen, to become something in himself, to become world, to become world for himself for another's sake.[4]

There is no avoiding the reality that pain is a part of every relationship. We are joined by our common experience of pain, find relief when our wounds "fit" each other like a key in a lock, quarrel when our wound is irritated, and become worthy and honorable opponents when we decide to accept the challenge of our joint wounding and take on the responsibility of our own ripening—and *for another's sake* as well as our own.

In marriage there is no escape from the dark corners of another human being. Days, weeks, even years after a hurtful word, you may still feel the ache of it beneath your ribs. Your spouse may set your teeth on edge the way a knife does when it scrapes over a plate. Just by the way he slops coffee on the kitchen counter; by his righteousness about the state of the world, about people who don't share his political views; by the way he says he loves you, grudgingly somehow, and only when you have said it first.

Ultimately, there is no escape from the mirror another casts on our own vulnerabilities. However exalted our intentions—however ready we may be to quote some spiritual wisdom from some great author or text—marriage, by design, offers us a context in which to see through the mirage of our own defenses. It summons not only the joy and delight of a shared life together but the fears, the resentments, the disillusion; the sheer difficulty that comes with the fact of being human.

Perhaps this is not the picture we thought we had signed up for. We may choose to live for years without seeing what is before our eyes; without our shell cracking open to allow the wellspring of a deeper love to flow through our days. After all, it requires sorrow as well as joy for those waters to flow; a sorrow that may include the recognition of our own loveless state, our own rigid stance toward the other and the world.

These tensions and struggles, both internal to us and shared with our partner, are part of what Denise Levertov is referring to in her poem "The Ache of Marriage." Yet the poem also infers that there is in marriage a treasure and a joy that can be found nowhere else. Perhaps it is the faint knowledge of this hidden gold that leads so many of us still to enter its gates, even in a time when half of all marriages dissolve in a few years.

For marriage is indeed an ark, as Levertov calls it later in her poem; even if it carries some of us only partway across life's ocean. It is an ark in which the very ache of being human can be revealed and also redeemed through a conscious undertaking shared with another. Throughout her poem, Levertov refers to her husband as "beloved." Even though

We look for communion
and are turned away, beloved,
each and each.

Even in the anguish of longing for communion with him and always
being turned away—not by her husband but by the fact that they will
forever be separate individuals, however close they come to each
other—even so, he remains her beloved.

This is the ebb and flow of intimacy: we draw close, we pull away,
because we all take part in the eternal dance of wanting to dissolve
into union and at the same time to affirm our individuality. In another
of her poems, Levertov says

Don't lock me in wedlock, I want
marriage, an
encounter—[5]

She doesn't want to be locked up in a merger. It is a meeting she
wants. An encounter requires two people. It calls for an aloneness-
in-togetherness. Even so, there is an ache in the realization that *even
between the closest people infinite distances exist.*

It's an ache that Clare Shaw, in her poem "Vow," is ready to bear.

Love did not turn from hurt
or hard work.
[. . .]
how love will insist with its ache,

[. . .]
How love must, at all costs,

be answered. . . .

She and her partner made a vow a long time ago. They stood up before their community and publicly acknowledged their responsibility toward this form—*this ark,* to return to Denise Levertov's evocative image of sanctuary and safe haven—that joins you with another human being within the constraints of time. To acknowledge your place in time is to surrender the fantasy of immortality and limitless possibilities. It is to admit to the limitations and gravity of the earth, to the wear and tear of life with feet of clay.

Shaw took all this on, and consciously, if we are to judge from her poem. The two of them have labored together, fought together, loved together, held each other

when nothing was given by right.

And now, after years of loving and struggling, they can still feel the current of their vows coursing below the surface of their days. Her poem is a celebration of their willingness to have labored and come through. On this day, she is as certain as she was on her wedding day that this is the man she will spend the rest of her life with:

So now I can tell you, quite simply
you are the house I will live in.

All that remains is for them to renew their vow and celebrate it in the light of the journey they have traveled:

   . . . Today, my love,
   rooms bloom with flowers.
   Say yes.
   The sky is ours.

Know Deeply, Know Thyself More Deeply

BY D. H. LAWRENCE

Go deeper than love, for the soul has greater depths,
love is like the grass, but the heart is deep wild rock
molten, yet dense and permanent.

Go down to your deep old heart, woman, and lose sight
    of yourself.
And lose sight of me, the me whom you turbulently loved.

Let us lose sight of ourselves, and break the mirrors.
For the fierce curve of our lives is moving again to the depths
out of sight, in the deep dark living heart.

The Well of Grief

BY DAVID WHYTE

Those who will not slip beneath
the still surface on the well of grief,

turning downward through its black water
to the place we cannot breathe,

will never know the source from which we drink,
the secret water, cold and clear,

nor find in the darkness glimmering,
the small round coins,
thrown by those who wished for something else.

The Ache of Marriage
BY DENISE LEVERTOV

The ache of marriage:

thigh and tongue, beloved,
are heavy with it,
it throbs in the teeth

We look for communion
and are turned away, beloved,
each and each

It is leviathan and we
in its belly
looking for joy, some joy
not to be known outside it

two by two in the ark of
the ache of it.

Vow

BY CLARE SHAW

Say yes.
That word on your lips
is a kiss;
is a promise already made.
We made it.

Love did not turn from hurt
or hard work.
When lights failed, it did not switch off.
When love had no road,
we willingly built it.

We shouldered its stones
and its dirt. So thank god
there are days like this when it's easy.
When we open our mouths
and the words flood in.

Put the word of your hand
in mine.

We have learnt to hold to each other
when nothing was given by right;
how love will insist with its ache,

with its first painful tug on the guts.
How love must, at all costs,

be answered. We have answered
and so have a million before us
and each of their names is a vow.
So now I can tell you, quite simply
you are the house I will live in:

there is no good reason
to move. Good earth,
you are home, stone, sun,
all my countries. Vital to me
as the light. You are it

and I am asking.
Say yes.

Love opens a door
then slams it. It does.
It loses its touch and its looks.
But love needs its fury.
We have fought

and when times make it necessary,
we will again. When night draws in,
we won't forget
how once the streets ran wet with light
and love. Like blood. They will again.

But for now,
we make our promises gently.
This extraordinary day we have made.
Listen—
the birds in their ordinary heaven.

Tonight the sky will blaze
with stars. Today, my love,
rooms bloom with flowers.
Say yes.
The sky is ours.

4

The Love

Awake awhile.
Just one true moment of Love
Will last for days.

——HAFIZ

❧ Wake Up and Love

THERE IS WISDOM IN the old marriage vows, the ones in the Book of Common Prayer, which speak of honoring and cherishing your beloved. (Those vows also include the word *obey*, which today we would see as a relic of an earlier age of the subjugation of women; although in its origins, the word meant *to listen*, which has a vital place for both marriage partners now as much as it ever did.) When you honor someone, you hold them in deep regard. When you cherish them, you value them; your heart goes out to them. You want what is best for them, regardless of what it might mean for you. Your love is based on your wish for their highest good, and not on your own self preservation. To cherish someone is to hold them in a loving regard; in a field of energy and attentiveness that nurtures. Anyone in a marriage or long-term relationship will be familiar with this field; though naturally it will be tested frequently by events and temperaments as you journey together through the years.

How does it feel to be in the warmth of a loving regard? Like a plant might feel as it turns toward the sun. Desire arises for the source of our desire. We want to be close to them, touch them, make love with them maybe, or simply hold their hand. I would say the heart door springs open, and some of our self-concern dissolves like mist in the morning light. Then, when we love another deeply, we engage the soul; and the soul, whose nature is relatedness, feels all things. We feel our partner's joy and also their pain; we feel the tension of their doubts and fears, the tenderness of their hopes and dreams. Not as codependents who have merged their identities but as two individuals who stand side by side in support of each other. A sustained loving is the work (as Rilke called it in the previous chapter) of an authentic individual; one who does not lose herself in the loving.

And because I do not always remember these truths; because there are sentinels who sometimes guard my own heart-door—my fears, my self-importance, meanness, greed, bitterness, and more— I often turn to poetry; because I have found that a good poem can sometimes slip past them all with a key to unlock my own deeper knowing.

We all need reminders to bring us back home to ourselves, and one such for me is "It Happens All the Time in Heaven," Daniel Ladinsky's version of some lines of Hafiz. Hafiz was the great fourteenth-century Persian poet and mystic whose verses are consulted still today on a daily basis by most everybody in Iran. What happens all the time in heaven, which the poet hopes will happen soon on earth, is that couples get down on their knees,

> . . . and while
> So tenderly holding their lover's hand, with
>
> Tear-filled eyes, will sincerely say, "My dear,
> How can I be more loving to you; my darling,
> How can I be more kind?"

Notice that the lover here has the simple humility to ask the question. We may not know exactly how our partner might wish us to express our love and also our kindness more explicitly. People have different needs. So we need to ask. We need to have that conversation. In saying that this kind of openheartedness happens all the time in heaven, Hafiz is reminding us how delicate and also subtle this field of loving regard really is. It is not automatic. It needs our careful attention. The heaven Hafiz refers to is nowhere if not here, now, always accessible deep in our own heart and soul.

When we feel loved, the deep heart can open. It can also open through sorrow. In her poem "Kindness," Naomi Shihab Nye says that

> Before you know kindness as the deepest thing inside,
> you must know sorrow as the other deepest thing.[1]

We ourselves may need to have suffered in life to be able to feel the sorrow of others. Empathy means being able to feel along with someone. We may have had some experience in our own lives that can help us appreciate their pain. If we can step outside of ourselves and exercise the faculty of our imagination, that too can join us to the heart of another in their time of need. When two people traverse difficulty and sorrow together, it may bring them closer or drive them apart. Which way they go will depend on how willing they are to keep their hearts open even in the darkest night.

Shakespeare, in his immortal "Sonnet 116," adds a further dimension to this subtle quality of love that Hafiz gives voice to. He declares that

> . . . Love is not love
> Which alters when it alteration finds.

The one thing we can be sure of is that we will change, and so will our partner. Shakespeare's sonnets themselves, whose general subject is love, pass through varying cycles of elation and depression. We may or may not develop different interests, have accelerated mood swings, be led into new areas of experience, or become attracted to other people. We will certainly grow older, lose our youthful glow, perhaps succumb to sickness, and eventually we will die. In his previous sonnet, 115, Shakespeare fully acknowledges the effects of

> Time, whose million'd accidents
> Creep in twixt vows, and change decrees of kings,
> Tan sacred beauty, blunt the sharps't intents,
> Divert strong minds to the course of alterning things . . .[2]

Even so, in "Sonnet 116" he says that

> Love's not time's fool, though rosy lips and cheeks
> Within his bending sickle's compass come.

We cannot avoid the inevitable changes that time will bring to us and to our relationship. A marriage, or any committed relationship, will never survive if its vows are fixed in tablets of stone. We need to be open to the unknown and the unexpected; for life itself is a grand unknown, an adventure and a mystery that only reveals itself as we continue the journey.

Yet love itself is beyond time and beyond conditions, Shakespeare says. It is a quality of being, a profound regard and caring for another that flows spontaneously from the couple's *true minds*. The term *true minds* is a reference to Plato, and his firm belief in the love and wisdom of a mind that lives in the heart, beyond the anxieties of the thinking brain and the vicissitudes of time. Unforeseen conditions may even force us to part at some stage; this true and exalted love, inherently not self-seeking, will continue to hold the other in deep regard, even in the deepest sorrow of parting or sickness.

Such a love as Shakespeare and Hafiz are describing, both selfless and eternal, was given the name *Agape* by the ancient Greeks. Plato himself considered this the most refined and lasting form of love, but it was accompanied by a more earthly counterpart, equally important, whose name is still legion today. It is Eros who brings a warmth and fire to your union, and especially when you nourish and cherish your shared dreams, delights, and joys. *Eros* is both our desire and the face of satisfied desire, the embodiment of our intimacy in the relative domain, whereas *Agape* is the vertical dimension of spirit. A lasting intimacy will need them both.

When we love one another, anything and everything we do can be a source of shared delight. Everything that is alive is humming with Eros, the god who gave his name to the passage of life that pours through all things. When we reel in delight at the fragrance of jasmine; when we stroke the cat or savor a fine wine; when we gaze in awe at the Acropolis in Athens, at a glorious sunset, or at our lover's face—it is all the trace of the invisible god who brings life and pleasure, the deep pleasure of soul food, to the tips of our fingers and the light in our eyes. Our sighs and gasps of satisfied desire, whatever may cause them, are the prayers Eros loves to feed on.

With Eros, we bring our love down to earth. Yet there will be times when the flame of Eros will falter and you will feel banished, like the original pair, from the garden. Love's flame may flicker for lack of time and air; when the pressing needs of family, or earning a living, crowd in upon your days. That is just when Eros longs to be invited back. If Eros is neglected too long, and weeks and months stretch into years, the flame that brought us together in the first place will eventually flicker and even die. Then the relationship itself will become a husk, a shell that is lived in merely for convenience or from fear of being alone.

Shared delights can range from the most exalted and ecstatic love-making to the humblest ordinary moments. One couple I know who have lived a lifetime together find a simple and yet profound pleasure in sitting next to each other on their sofa in silence and simply rubbing each other's feet. Stroking, touching, fondling—it doesn't come much simpler than that. The accumulation of small, apparently insignificant acts of love and kindness like this can serve to carry the flame of the relationship down through the years.

We are mammals, after all, none of us so very far from preening chimps, and touch is one of our basic needs. If you notice you are not touching each other as much as you used to—a hug, a kiss, a hand on a shoulder even—you might see it as a sign that a distance has come between you, a distance you may not even have been aware of. A simple touch can bridge that distance. It can give life again to the flame between you. We human beings need the light of Eros—whose other name is love—if we are to be anything more than *a bent penny or a scuffed shoe*, as Mary Oliver would say.

Too often we associate the name of *Eros* solely with sexual delight, and while it's true that sex is one of the greatest playing fields of the Lord of Love, Eros takes pleasure in all the myriad ways two lovers can share beauty and joy. Whatever we share with our beloved that brings us genuine pleasure will fan the flames of love. A shared pleasure is an intimacy, something that brings us closer than we were a moment before. It may be subtle, it may be thrilling—Chopin or Beethoven, the soft light of dusk or a thunderstorm—but it will never be merely skin deep. A genuine pleasure will move us, stir us, leave a tremor of delight on the tongue, in the eyes, or echoing in the ears. Eros likes whatever is food for the soul—after all, he fell in love with Psyche, whose very name gave us the notion of soul. All he needs is for us to give him the time of day.

Stephen Dunn's poem *I Came Home Wanting to Touch Everyone* could be a song of praise to the god of love. Eros is at home in all of our senses, but none more than our sense of touch. It is our capacity to touch, after all, that brings us into direct and bodily contact with the world. Even to hold something as seemingly lifeless as a stone, to turn it over and rub it between thumb and forefinger, can induce a sense of calm and ease. An exchange begins to grow between stone and hand; and a simple, wordless intimacy—intimacy in the sense of a passage of warmth from one object or being to another—can emerge between us and the speck of earth in our hand.

That passage of warmth is a flow of Eros, and when it passes between people who love one another it goes to affirm their love. It makes it tangible, brings it out into the open; gives it expression in form. So when Stephen Dunn opens his front door and his dogs come bounding up to him, all paws and panting tongues, nothing could be more natural than for him to *descend into their world of fur and tongues. . . .*

It gets even better when his wife greets him, and they

> . . . embrace
> as if we'd just closed the door
> in a motel, our two girls slip in
> between us and we're all saying
> each other's names and the dogs
> Buster and Sundown are on their hind legs,
> people-style, seeking more love.

Not that it's always this way. As he says in the poem, he usually opens the door and everyone is absorbed in their different worlds—his wife is busy making dinner, his girls are deep in their homework, the dogs are busy with each other. Ordinary family life, in other words, as it is known and experienced up and down the country. Back from work, he, the male provider, lets himself in and fixes himself a drink and looks at the mail. This is not a newlywed couple. They have already traversed enough years to gather a family and settle into a routine that would be recognized by millions. Even so, this poem shows that they are not entirely lost in the routine. The flame still sputters on, just waiting for a breath of air to bring it to life again. As Dunn puts it,

> . . . love itself has risen
> from its squalor of neglect.

Because we do neglect our love. Life takes over, especially when the couple grows into a family. It can be all too easy to forget that a few moments of shared delight in whatever form it may take for us is as important—more important, in the long run—as discussing the bill that still needs to be paid. Our love is a flower, and it needs to be tended.

What Stephen Dunn notices is that this spontaneous awakening of warmth and his wanting to touch everyone is contagious. For him it moves from the sensual to the sexual—a natural and delightful extension—and as soon as his kids turn their backs his hands move to his wife's breasts. Even the cat, who is usually so unfriendly, begins to purr and *wants to rub heads* and the whole household is lit up with the feeling of satisfied desire. For

> . . . everyone is intelligible
> in the language of touch,
> and we sit down to dinner inarticulate
> as blood, all difficulties postponed
> because the weather is so good.

Love is like that. It doesn't always need words. It can spread out like a fan, beyond even the couple itself, forming a field in which others too are made good and made whole. The love Stephen Dunn catches with his pen and gets onto paper is not of the mind. It speaks the language of touch, which may seem inarticulate but has an intelligence that our hearts and our bodies understand without the intermediary of words. In the embrace of this love, he says, all difficulties are postponed.

All difficulties are postponed for the young couple in Carol Tufts's poem "We Take the New Young Couple Out to Dinner":

> They go at it in the backseat of our car,
> Then on into the restaurant,

And later out on the sidewalk,
Their snatching hands all over each other
So wc will see the heat flashing between them
Like the neon in a splashy marquee.

There is nothing like love-making—a few moments or hours of trans-port out of oneself—to dissolve the worries of daily existence; to bring a couple close to each other, not merely in a physical exchange but in an emotional intimacy, at least for the duration of the love-making itself. This, it is often assumed, is the natural territory of the young, which older couples are more likely only to remember wist-fully from their own earlier days together.

Tufts, in her poem, appears to be setting up a poignant contrast between the young couple and the older couple who are taking them out to dinner, whom she describes as

A blunted old-married couple,
The wistful audience
Before their flickering screen.

They are not old so much as old-married—they have been together a long time, in contrast to their dinner guests, who seem to be near the beginning of their adventure into love. The word *blunted* suggests that the older couple have long since lost the fire of their sexual attrac-tion for each other, somewhere down through the years of navigating life's difficulties together. But like many good poems, this one takes a surprising turn. The young lovers would never dream what the older pair is thinking as they traipse into the restaurant behind them. They are thinking of the monkey island at the zoo; all that preening and *fingering one another's pelts*.

And the reader imagines that the image comes from looking, perhaps enviously, certainly *wistfully*, at the sensual fire and joy of the young couple in front of them. But no, for

> When we say our tactful goodnights,
> What they would never think is
> How we will unlock the doors
> Of our own modest house
> And with you hard
> Behind me, your hands clasping
> My swaying hips,
> Feel our way, breathless,
> Through the jungle dark.

I love how Tufts turns her poem round on her readers and defies their expectations. I love how this older couple returns home feeling their primal way *through the jungle dark*. Contrary to conventional wisdom, sensual desire can fan the flame between two people for decades, and especially if they have nurtured it with acts of common kindness and joy.

While the first two poems in this section remind us to keep our connection to spirit alive, to affirm together a love beyond all conditions, the poems by Stephen Dunn and Carol Tufts remind us how important it is to keep the flame of desire alive as well. Both Agape and

Eros, each in their different ways, serve to nourish a deep and lasting relationship. Making love, delighting in dinner together, or simply sitting in a shared silence that leads to a communion of spirit—no matter what we do, what matters is that we wake up and love in all the ways that we can.

It Happens All the Time in Heaven
BY HAFIZ *translation by Daniel Ladinsky*

It happens all the time in heaven, and someday
It will begin to happen again on earth—

That men and women who are married, and
Men and women who are lovers,

And women and women who give each other
Light,

Often will get down on their knees, and while
So tenderly holding their lover's hand, with

Tear-filled eyes, will sincerely say, "My dear,
How can I be more loving to you; my darling,
How can I be more kind?"

Sonnet 116

BY WILLIAM SHAKESPEARE

Let me not to the marriage of true minds
Admit impediments. Love is not love
Which alters when it alteration finds,
Or bends with the remover to remove:
O no! it is an ever-fixed mark,
That looks on tempests and is never shaken;
It is the star to every wandering bark,
Whose worth's unknown, although his height be taken.
Love's not Time's fool, though rosy lips and cheeks
Within his bending sickle's compass come:
Love alters not with his brief hours and weeks,
But bears it out even to the edge of doom.
If this be error and upon me proved,
I never writ, nor no man ever loved.

I Come Home Wanting to Touch Everyone
BY STEPHEN DUNN

The dogs greet me, I descend
into their world of fur and tongues
and then my wife and I embrace
as if we'd just closed the door
in a motel, our two girls slip in
between us and we're all saying
each other's names and the dogs
Buster and Sundown are on their hind legs,
people-style, seeking more love.
I've come home wanting to touch
everyone, everything; usually I turn
the key and they're all lost
in food or homework, even the dogs
are preoccupied with themselves,
I desire only to ease
back in, the mail, a drink,
but tonight the body-hungers have sent out
their long-range signals
or love itself has risen
from its squalor of neglect.
Everytime the kids turn their backs
I touch my wife's breasts
and when she checks the dinner

the unfriendly cat on the dishwasher
wants to rub heads, starts to speak
with his little motor and violin—
everything, everyone is intelligible
in the language of touch,
and we sit down to dinner inarticulate
as blood, all difficulties postponed
because the weather is so good.

We Take the New Young Couple Out to Dinner
BY CAROL TUFTS

They go at it in the backseat of our car,
Then on into the restaurant,
And later out on the sidewalk,
Their snatching hands all over each other
So we will see the heat flashing between them
Like the neon in a splashy marquee
Above a theater they would have us enter
A blunted old-married couple,
The wistful audience
Before their flickering screen.
What they would never think is
How we are thinking just now
Of monkey island at the zoo,
The meticulous chimps
Fingering one another's pelts,
Browsing for fleas, the lone baboon
Masturbating to beat the band.
And still at it
When we say our tactful goodnights,
What they would never think is
How we will unlock the doors
Of our own modest house

And with you hard
Behind me, your hands clasping
My swaying hips,
Feel our way, breathless,
Through the jungle dark.

5

The Union

> When two people walk far enough into
> The distance they merge.
>
> ——CZESLAW MILOSZ

❧ Not One, Not Two

THE UNION THAT COUPLES MAY ENJOY in later life may well
have been there in seed form all along. The first flush of love colors the
cheeks when two people recognize something in each other beyond
mere outer appearances. A true union takes place in the realm of the
soul, and often it is the soul that recognizes the other in the early days
of love.

The union that usually, though not always, takes a long time to
forge is a deeply shared common purpose that lies beyond the couple's
individual needs. It is beyond the demands of survival, of children, and
of security. It is the actualization of what Kahlil Gibran, in his poem in
the second section, alludes to in his beautiful image of the two pillars
that together hold up the temple. In this union, the couple is not one, in
the sense of being merged. Yet they are not two, either; not separate and
apart from each other. They live and breathe together in the embrace
of something greater than themselves, which in Gibran's image is the
temple itself. Yet without them, the temple would not exist.

The temple is a third thing, and it is not difficult to see some anal-
ogy in the Christian idea of the Holy Spirit. It is what breathes life into
the relationship, inspires it, uplifts it. Its other name is Love. Not love
of this or that in the other, but, as we have called it before, a field of
love that nourishes both partners, raises them up to the best that they
are, and makes good that which may have been lost in the shadows.
There is a peace in this quality of union, a peace that is alive. It is the

restfulness of coming home—not only to the other so much as to this third place, which Robert Bly calls "A Third Body."

This has been one of my best-loved poems for decades. At first glance "A Third Body" might not be what you would normally associate with a love poem. After all, there seems to be no ardor, no passion, nothing happening. But that is the point: in the stillness, the coolness of it, it carries the quiet intensity of a new moon.

The man and the woman in this poem do not long for anything other than what they have in this moment. It is an uncommon state, the soul not wanting to leap out of the body in pursuit of some passing thought or fleeting desire, but content to be where it is, speaking or not speaking. In this moment, the search for some better conditions, better options, better understanding even, is over. They do not long

> at this moment to be older, or younger, nor born
> in any other nation, or time, or place.
> They are content to be where they are, talking or
>   not-talking.

Being where they are in the simplicity and the fullness of the moment is entirely sufficient. Imagine the deep rest that is inherent in such a condition; how rare it is in this worried and agitated world. This is the temple this couple lives in.

Rumi writes often of this quality of being. It is an arc of love that is both of this world and not of it at the same time. Lovers can read his poetry and know that Rumi is speaking directly to them. Lovers of the divine can read the same lines and know the same thing. Bly's poem reminds me of one Rumi poem in particular, called "This We Have Now." Our feelings and moods come and go, Rumi says, but

This is the presence
That doesn't.[1]

It is the presence that Bly's couple shares. You may know this quiet, in which life seems to live itself, and you can rest in the simplicity of watching it unfold.

he sees her hand close around a book she hands to him.

Anything within the field of this presence—even the gesture of a hand closing around a book—can assume a substance beyond its normal means. You may know this in your own life—a moment, an hour, when the air you share with your beloved is charged, whether you are speaking or not speaking, and every gesture seems effortless, weightless even.

This is the flavor of the third body. The nature of this love is itself a sacrament. Bly tells us twice in the poem that the couple is sitting near each other, as if to impress upon us that they are not in physical contact. They do not need to be. They are feeling each other through the third body that exists between them. Their love does not deny physical love, but it does not need it either. Perhaps their shared presence will lead to making love. Or perhaps it won't. There is neither any desire nor any fear of desire anywhere in the poem. This couple breathes a subtler air.

The knowledge of this presence is built into the fabric of our being human; so we can feel the tremor of it in a poem even if we have not actually experienced it in our lives. This is why so many of us live with a longing for a love that encompasses both worlds. You can only long for something, after all, if you know in your bones that it must already exist.

The love in Bly's poem is what I have called Agape in the previous section. It carries the signature of the spirit. But the warmer love of Eros is also part of a joyous, more earthly union; it can be a sign not just of a first flush of ardor but an ongoing delight in one's partner. It would be a mistake to think that such warmth and enjoyment in each other inevitably pales with the passing of the years. Fran Landesman's poem *Come with Me* could equally have been written to her partner at the beginning of their relationship or after decades had passed. She was married to Jan Landesman for sixty years, and they led a rich and colorful life.

Her poem in this section burns with her delight in her beloved. She wants to do everything with him, experience everything, the lows as well as the highs, with him, pray with him, sin with him, live life in all its colors with him. She wants to do all of this so completely, so utterly, that there can be nothing left of her that is hers alone.

Nothing is mine now, it's ours.

Her poem is an ecstatic song of praise to the electricity and joy that can flow between two people who are in rhythm and resonance. It is another kind of third body, neither less than nor more than Bly's quieter body of presence. Fran's is an electric, dancing, joyous body—a soul body rather than a spirit body—that sings a song made for two.

In his quieter way, I suspect that Wendell Berry must have heard something of that same song when he wrote "The Blue Robe." Again, he echoes the theme of Gibran's pillars and temple in the first line,

How joyful to be together, alone

His poem is the fruit of a lifetime of marriage, in which there has been a gradual fruition of their intimacy, so that now, late in life,

. . . we belong to one story
that the two, joining, made. . . .

They know they are mortal now, toward the end of their lives, which makes their love all the more tender. And yet still, he says,

how joyful to feel the heart quake
at the sight of a grandmother,
old friend in the morning light,
beautiful in her blue robe!

How beautiful, and also tender, to read such lines by one who has lived so many decades with his beloved. Still, even after all these years, his heart quakes at the sight of his wife, now a grandmother, always his *old friend*, lovely as ever in his eyes. Truly, as Hafiz says in the final poem, "Nothing Can Shatter This Love." May it be so for your love, you who have come almost to the end of these pages. All that remains after the poems on The Union is The Saving Grace. You never know when you may need it.

A Third Body

BY ROBERT BLY

A man and a woman sit near each other, and they do
    not long
at this moment to be older, or younger, nor born
in any other nation, or time, or place.
They are content to be where they are, talking or
    not-talking.
Their breaths together feed someone whom we do not
    know.
The man sees the way his fingers move;
he sees her hands close around a book she hands to him.
They obey a third body that they share in common.
They have promised to love that body.
Age may come, parting may come, death will come.
A man and a woman sit near each other;
as they breathe they feed someone we do not know,
someone we know of, whom we have never seen.

Come with Me
BY FRAN LANDESMAN

Come with me, go with me, burn with me, glow with me,
Write me a sonnet or two
Sleep with me, wake with me, give with me, take with me
Love me the way I love you.

Let me get high with you, laugh with you, cry with you,
Be with you when I am blue
Rest with you, fight with you, day with you, night with you,
Love me whatever I do.

Work with me, play with me, run with me, stay with me
Make me your partner in crime
Handle me, fondle me, cradle me tenderly
Say I'm your reason and rhyme
Pray with me, sin with me, lose with me, win with me
Love me with all of my scars
Rise with me, fall with me, hide from it all with me
Nothing is mine now, it's ours.

The Blue Robe

BY WENDELL BERRY

How joyful to be together, alone
as when we first were joined
in our little house by the river
long ago, except that now we know
each other, as we did not then;
and now instead of two stories fumbling
to meet, we belong to one story
that the two, joining, made. And now
we touch each other with the tenderness
of mortals, who know themselves:
how joyful to feel the heart quake
at the sight of a grandmother,
old friend in the morning light,
beautiful in her blue robe!

Nothing Can Shatter This Love
BY HAFIZ *translation by Daniel Ladinsky*

Nothing can shatter this love,
For even if you took another

into your arms, the truth is,
my sweetheart, you would
still
be
kissing
Me.

6

The Saving Grace

There is a crack, a crack in everything.
That's how the light gets in.

——LEONARD COHEN

From *Listening to the Köln Concert*
BY ROBERT BLY

When men and women come together,
how much they have to abandon! Wrens
make their nests of fancy threads
and string ends, animals

abandon all their money each year.
What is it that men and women leave?
Harder than wrens' doing, they have
to abandon their longing for the perfect.

The inner nest not made by instinct
will never be quite round,
and each has to enter the nest
made by the other imperfect bird.

Notes

The Recognition

1. Henry Corbin, *Alone with the Alone: Creative Imagination in the Sufism of Ibn 'Arabi* (Princeton, N.J.: Princeton University Press, 1998), 111.

Soaked in Honey, Stung and Swollen

1. Ellen Bass, "If You Knew," in *The Human Line* (Port Townsend, Wash.: Copper Canyon Press, 2007), 51.
2. Rainer Maria Rilke, *Letters of Rainer Maria Rilke Volume 1: 1892–1910,* trans. Jane Bannard and M. D. Herter Norton (New York: W. W. Norton, 1945), 152.
3. Rainer Maria Rilke, *Letters to a Young Poet,* trans. S. Mitchell (New York: Random House, 1984), 68.
4. Rainer Maria Rilke, *Rilke on Love and Other Difficulties,* trans. John J. L. Mood (New York: W. W. Norton, 1975), 31.
5. Denise Levertov, "About Marriage," in *Poems 1960–1967* (New York: New Directions, 1983), 140.

Wake Up and Love

1. Naomi Shihab Nye, "Kindness," in *Words under the Words: Selected Poems* (Portland, Ore.: The Eighth Mountain Press, 1995), 32.
2. William Shakespeare, *The Sonnets* (New York: Little, Brown, 1998), 115.

Not One, Not Two

1. Rumi, "This We Have Now," in *Rumi: The Book of Love,* trans. Coleman Barks (San Francisco: HarperSanFrancisco, 2003), 182.

About the Poets

CONRAD AIKEN (1889–1973)

Aiken was born in Savannah, Georgia. When he was still a small boy his father killed his mother and then committed suicide, an event that deeply marked the young boy's life. Aiken was brought up by a great-great aunt in Massachusetts and went to Harvard in 1912, the same time as T. S. Eliot and E. E. Cummings. His first collection of poetry, *Earth Triumphant,* was published in 1914 and quickly established his reputation as a poet. Much of his poetry reflects a deep interest in psychoanalysis and the development of identity. He published thirty-three volumes of poetry, including his *Collected Poems,* which won the National Book Award in 1953. As the editor of Emily Dickinson's *Selected Poetry,* published in 1924, Aiken was largely responsible for establishing her posthumous literary celebrity.

WENDELL BERRY (B. 1934)

Berry, a farmer with an intense interest in man's relationship to the land and in sustainable living, lives in his native Kentucky. He is the author of more than thirty books of poetry, essays, and novels. A reviewer for the *Christian Science Monitor* has written that "Berry's poems shine with the gentle wisdom of a craftsman who has thought deeply about the paradoxical strangeness and wonder of life."

ROBERT BLY (B. 1926)

Bly is a poet, editor, translator, storyteller, and father of what he has called "the expressive men's movement." He was born in Minnesota to parents of Norwegian stock. In 1956 he went to Norway on a Fulbright scholarship to translate Norwegian poetry into English. He returned to start a literary review, *The Fifties* and then *The Sixties* and *The Seventies,* which introduced these poets to his generation. During the 1970s he had eleven books of poetry, essays, and translations published, with four more appearing in the 1980s. His most recent collection is *My Sentence Was a Thousand Years of Joy,* published in 2005.

Roy Croft (1856–1917)

Croft was an Australian-born lumber and mining magnate who lived on Vancouver Island in Canada in the early 1900's. He founded the town of Crofton in 1902 as a place to house the smelter for his coal mine on Mount Sicker. Croft was not a published poet, and whether he was actually the original writer of this poem is not known, although authorship is popularly ascribed to him. The version in this book is my own adaptation.

Stephen Dunn (b. 1939)

Dunn served in the military, played professional basketball, and worked as an advertising executive before settling into a career of writing and academic teaching at a variety of universities, a career that has continued to the present time. In *Poetry* magazine, David Baker wrote that Stephen Dunn "brings reports from the nearly paralyzed districts of American suburbia and middle age." He does so in unadorned, conversational language that always tends to the insight that life has value not only despite but also because of the concerns and little mediocrities of everyday life. He has published eleven poetry collections, one of which, *Different Hours,* won the Pulitzer Prize in 2000.

Kahlil Gibran (1883–1931)

Gibran was born into a Christian Maronite family in Lebanon. His father gambled and drank, and eventually ended up in jail, leaving the family poverty-stricken. Gibran had no formal education, but a local priest taught him Arabic and some Greek and infused in him an awareness of the mystical dimensions of Maronite Christianity. When he was eight, his mother moved the family to Boston, and Gibran's education began in earnest as the result of a scholarship, revealing early on his gifts for art and poetry. He went to Paris in 1909 to broaden his art training, and on his return to the United States a couple of years later he began to publish Arabic prose poetry. In 1911 he moved to New York, and it was there that he painted his portrait of Carl Jung. During World War I he published *The Prophet,* which has continued to be an international best seller ever since. He died of cancer at the age of forty-eight.

Eliza Griswold (b. 1973)

Griswold is a Nieman Fellow journalist and foreign correspondent who has reported extensively for the *New Yorker, Atlantic Monthly,* the *New York Times Magazine,* and

Harper's. Her *NewYork Times* best-selling book *The Tenth Parallel* examines the relation-ship between Islam and Christianity along the tenth parallel, which runs through Nigeria, Sudan, Indonesia, and Malaysia. Her first book of poems, *Wideawake Field*, was published by Farrar, Strauss and Giroux in 2007, and in 2010 she won the Rome Prize for poetry from the American Academy. She is a senior fellow at the New America Foundation.

Shams-Ud-Din Muhammad Hafiz (c. 1320–89)

Goethe was one of the first Westerners to discover Hafiz, whom he considered "a poet for poets." Emerson found Hafiz through Goethe's work, and did several translations of his own into English. The complete collection of his poems, the *Diwan-i-Hafiz,* still sells more copies today in his native Persia than any other book. Hafiz was born and lived in the city of Shiraz. Of lowly stock, he worked as a baker's assistant by day and put himself through school at night. Over many years he mastered the subjects of a classical medieval education, which included the great Persian poets. During middle age, Hafiz served as a court poet. By the time he was sixty, he had become famous for his inspired verses, and he became both a spiritual and literary teacher. Daniel Ladinsky has popularized his work in English with his versions that, while not literal translations, convey the spirit of this spiritual revolutionary.

Fran Landesman (1927–2011)

Landesman was a songwriter, poet, and performer who was born and grew up in New York City. She went to art school there, and spent a lot of her time in Green-wich Village, where she befriended the emerging Beat poets. Jack Kerouac was enamored of her, but in 1949 she met Jay Landesman, a magazine editor and bon vivant. Despite a wild and unconventional lifestyle, they were to stay together for the rest of their lives. One of Fran's songs, "Spring Can Really Hang You Up," was frequently covered in the 1950s by Ella Fitzgerald, Barbra Streisand, and others. In 1964 the Landesmans moved to London and immediately became a part of the flower power creative world there. They were to live there for the rest of their lives. In 1994 Landesman met the English composer Simon Wallace and launched into a new burst of activity that produced more than 350 new songs, three collections of poetry, and a full-blown musical.

D. H. LAWRENCE (1885–1930)

Lawrence was an acclaimed English novelist, short-story writer, essayist, and poet. Though better known for his novels, his first published works in 1909 were poems, and his poetry, especially his evocations of the natural world, has had a significant influence on poets on both sides of the Atlantic. A writer with radical views, Lawrence regarded sex, the primitive subconscious, and nature as cures for what he saw to be the evils of modern industrial society. A lifelong sufferer of tuberculosis, he died in 1930 in France.

DENISE LEVERTOV (1923–97)

Levertov's first book, *The Double Image,* which she wrote between the ages of seventeen and twenty-one, was published in 1946. Soon after emigrating from England to the United States, she was recognized as an important voice in the American avant-garde. Her next book, *With Eyes at the Back of Our Heads,* established her as one of the great American poets, and her English origins were forgotten. She published more than twenty volumes of poetry, and from 1989 to 1993 she taught at Stanford University. She spent the last decade of her life in Seattle. She was always an outsider, in England, in America, and also in poetry circles, for she never considered herself part of any school. She once said, "I nevertheless experience the sense of difference as an honor, as part of knowing at an early age that I was an artist-person and had a destiny."

WESLEY MCNAIR (B. 1941)

McNair, who lives in Mercer, Maine, is often referred to as a "poet of place." His work captures the lives of ordinary New Englanders by using his own life to explore family conflicts and other autobiographical subjects. He has written several volumes of poetry, including most recently *Lovers of the Lost: New and Collected Poems,* which came out in 2010. The poet Philip Levine has called him one of the great storytellers of contemporary poetry. McNair has been a teacher for many years, and is currently writer-in-residence at the University of Maine, Farmington.

HENRIK NORDBRANDT (B. 1945)

Nordbrandt's place in Danish literature is unique. He has spent most of his life abroad, in Turkey, Greece, and Italy. His poetry is imbued with the towns, land-scapes, and climates of the Mediterranean region; its colors, lights, and shadows. His first publication, *Poetry,* came out in 1966. Since the 1970s, he has been the leading poet of his generation, even though he never joined the then prevailing trend of writing easily accessible and socially engaged verse. He has published more than twenty volumes of poetry, including *Dream Bridges,* which won the Nordic Council's prestigious prize in 2000. He has also written a novel, a children's book, and a Turk-ish cookbook.

RUMI (1207–73)

Rumi was the founder of the Sufi order known as the Mevlevi (Whirling Dervishes) in Konya, Turkey. Though the theme of lover and beloved was already established in Sufi teaching, his own poetry was inspired by his meeting and the consequent loss of his great teacher, Shams of Tabriz. From their relationship was born some of the most inspired love poetry ever, in which Rumi sings of a love that is both personal and divine at the same time. After Shams's death, he would burst into ecstatic poetry anywhere, anytime, and his scribe disciple, Husam, was charged with writing it all down. Rumi's great spiritual treatise, *The Mathnawi,* written in couplets, amounts to more than twenty-five thousand lines in six books.

WILLIAM SHAKESPEARE (1564–1616)

Shakespeare is widely considered to be the greatest playwright the world has ever known, and the finest writer of any kind in the English language. He wrote 38 plays, 154 sonnets, and 2 long narrative poems. He was also an actor, a founding member of the acting troupe *The King's Men,* and a business partner in their theater, the Globe, in London. He married Anne Hathaway in his hometown of Stratford on Avon when he was just eighteen, but soon moved to London to start his career, leaving his wife and three children in Stratford. He was respected in his own time, but it was only in the nineteenth century that Shakespeare's reputation achieved the iconic status it still enjoys all over the world today. His sonnets were published in one volume in 1609.

CLARE SHAW (B. 1972)

Shaw was born in Burnley, in the north of England, the youngest of six children. She spent ten years in Liverpool, where she studied politics. Her years in the city were marked by frequent admissions to psychiatric wards, which motivated her to become involved in working to improve mental health services. She is gaining a reputation as one of the UK's most dynamic and powerful young poets. Her first volume, *Straight Ahead,* was published in 2006, and her new collection, *Head On*, was published by Bloodaxe Books in 2012. She currently lives with her young daughter and three cats by the canal in the market town of Todmorden, outside Manchester.

CAROL TUFTS (B. 1947)

Tufts teaches in the English Department of Oberlin College. Her poems have appeared, or are forthcoming, in a number of literary magazines, including *Poetry, Poet Lore, Iconoclast,* and *Poetica*. She is a recipient of an Individual Artist Award from the Ohio Arts Council and is at work on a first volume of poems.

DAVID WHYTE (B. 1955)

Whyte was born and raised in the North of England, studied marine zoology in Wales, and trained as a naturalist in the Galapagos Islands. He now lives in the Pacific Northwest with his wife and two children, and works full-time as a poet, reading and lecturing throughout the world. He is one of the few poets to bring his insights to bear on organizational life, working with corporations at home and abroad. He has published several volumes of poetry and has also written the best-selling prose books *Crossing the Unknown Sea: Work as a Pilgrimage of Identity* and *The Three Marriages: Re-Imagining Work, Self, and Relationship.*

Permissions